Career Construction
Counseling Manual

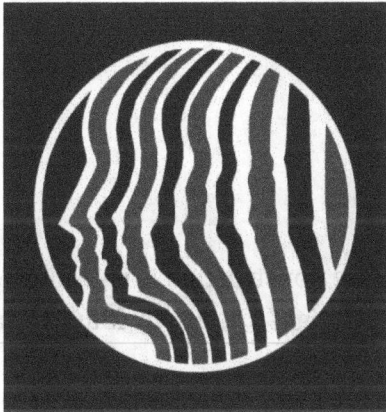

Mark L. Savickas

Table of Contents

Chapter One

Career Construction Counseling

The *Career Construction Counseling Manual* presents a principle-driven intervention that counselors may use to assist clients make career transitions. My primary purpose in writing this *Manual* was to enable graduate students and practitioners to develop the knowledge and skills involved in narrative counseling for career construction. Simply stated the *Manual* explains how counselors may become even more intentional in using narrative interventions to prompt client transformation. My second goal was to aid researchers improve coherence with the career construction counseling model when they conduct treatment studies.

This *Manual* presents a protocol for Career Construction Counseling (CCC) that describes phases of treatment, session-by-session principles, and an outline of procedures. Each component includes clearly defined yet flexible steps for common, everyday practice. The counseling techniques and strategies are concrete, specific, and illustrated with client examples. Although structured and systematic, the flexible guidelines allow counselors to appropriately address their clients' situations and values. Rather than mechanistically apply the guidelines, counselors use them to the extent that they correspond to a client's situation and needs.

Determining how to adapt the intervention to fit a particular client is the creative part. Counselors must assess what is useful in moving clients toward their goals. Career construction counselors improvise within a map of action. As a metaphor, I liken career construction counseling to jazz. One cannot play jazz without the notes, yet jazz musicians do not play the notes as written. Instead, they use the notes creatively and sometimes play between the notes. Responsive counselors who know the CCC discourse and its methods may confidently improvise to meet the needs of a specific client. In the words of Picasso, "Learn the rules like a professional, so you can break them like an artist."

Where do the notes for CCC come from? The guiding principles and intervention protocol are informed in general by the Career Construction Theory of vocational behavior and development (Savickas, 2002, 2020). They are informed in particular by practice-based evidence that includes client feedback, clinical observations, and published case studies. This *Manual* does not imply that the intervention methods are based on research evidence or proven outcomes. Rather, it details best practices of counseling for career construction drawn from analyses of case studies and derived from the collective experience of its practitioners.

Practice leads theory, not the other way around. As the social organization of work evolves and career trajectories change, counselors must respond to client needs before theory has time to address them. This means that counseling models emerge from practice, rather than from theory (Davies & Harre, 1990). Model making is different from theory building. In applied psychology, theorizing aims to explain a phenomenon by formulating a set of statements developed through a process of continued scientific measurement, experimentation, or prediction. In the counseling profession a model is a discursive device meant to systematize practice-based knowledge. Accordingly, Career Construction Theory as a part of applied psychology attempts to explain the phenomenon of vocational behavior and its development. In comparison, the CCC model as part of the counseling profession presents a discourse that formalizes and systematizes narrative interventions in the practice of career counseling.

Guidance Compared to Construction

Beginning in 1909 with the foundational model-making of Frank Parson, counselors have produced multifaceted discourses with a myriad of procedures that structure distinct interventions and services including vocational guidance, academic advising, career education, job placement, career development, career coaching, vocational rehabilitation, and career constructing (Savickas, 2015a).

For the purposes herein, I wish merely to differentiate between the practice of vocational guidance based on scores and CCC based on stories. Vocational guidance rests on logical positivism. This discourse positions counselors as subjects and clients as objects. Vocational guidance measures clients' objective resemblance to prototypes and occupational groups in terms of essentialist categories such as abilities, interests, and personality traits. CCC as a disciplinary discourse prefers a double hermeneutic (Rennie, 2012) in that it positions both client and counselor as subjects. Rather than test scores that indicate who clients resemble, CCC uses stories that show clients' uniqueness. To give a different account of clients, CCC assesses constructionist categories such as intention, purpose, and calling (Madigan, 2011). In short, guiding concentrates on scores whereas constructing concentrates on stories.

To learn more about the difference between guidance and constructing see Savickas (2012, 2015a). Herein it is sufficient to state that both vocational guidance and CCC are important interventions yet they differ markedly. The skilled practitioner can enact either discourse, depending upon client needs. Counselors realize that to be an expert, they must know their discipline from more than a single discourse; and to be competent they must be able to provide multiple services and apply various interventions. Thus, CCC is meant to take its place alongside vocational guidance, not replace it.

When counselors inhabit and apply a specific discourse, whether it be vocational guidance, career education, or CCC, they step on a semantic path laid down for a particular purpose and formed by specific principles and practices. The path of CCC discourse sets out by defining career as a story that a person tells about her or his working life. Because we live in language, that story imposes meaning on vocational choice and work behavior. CCC follows the path of a meaning-making dialogue between client and counselor to first encourage clients to narrate a career story with continuity and coherence and then prompt clients to engage in adaptive action in pursuit of a life that they want to live.

This *Manual* linguistically describes and operationally defines the purpose and principles of CCC practices for empowering clients to construct their careers. Clients and counselors move down the path of this manual-guided intervention as they form relationships to collaboratively address career concerns and resolve work-role problems.

Rationale for Using Narratives

People use stories to organize their lives, construct their identities, and make sense of their problems. Clients enter counseling with a story to tell about some transition. The stories people tell have a way of taking care of them. By holding those stories in the relationship, counselors enable clients to reflect on their lives. Dwelling in their own stories often destabilizes old ideas that block decision making and enables an awareness that prompts a choice. As clients

4

give voice to their stories, they hear what they already know and find the answers that they seek. From their own knowing emerges a new perspective that enables clients to revise their career stories. The vantage point of the new perspective enables clients to elaborate or change their stories in ways that clarify choices and prompt transformative actions to bridge the transition.

As outlined in Table 1, the process of CCC follows a standard sequence, one similar to Kolb's (1984) experiential learning cycle and Watson and Rennie's (1994) model of client operations. The process begins with addressing a client's tension by constructing micro-narratives that provide symbolic representations of concrete experience. This is followed by deconstruction of limiting ideas and self-negating beliefs with attention concentrated on reflective observation and self-examination. The third step produces new intentions by reconstructing a macro-narrative with abstract conceptualizations that beget new realizations. And finally, client and counselor co-construct an action plan that extends revisioning of the self through active experimentation in the real world.

Table 1. Outline of Sequence for CCC

Client Experience	Career Constructing (Savickas, 2019)	Learning Cycle (Kolb, 1984)	Client Operations (Watson & Rennie, 1994)
Tension	Construct	Concrete experience	Symbolic representation
Attention	Deconstruct	Reflective observation	Reflexive self-examination
Intention	Reconstruct	Abstract conceptualization	New realizations
Extension	Co-construct	Active experimentation	Revisioning self

Core Elements

In CCC, the core elements are a relationship, reflection, and sense-making. Career construction practitioners are experts on forming relationships, prompting reflection, and encouraging sense-making. They have the competence to facilitate client sense-making through the organization and reorganization of experience. They realize that a collaborative relationship provides a holding environment for this sense-making. And in this safe space, counselors know how to prompt client self-reflection to produce intentionality for the task of career reconstruction.

Relationship

Before the first meeting, clients may worry about whether the counselor will judge them, mistreat them, or be unable to help them. That is why the first goal of counseling is to establish a relationship. CCC involves two experts who form an egalitarian collaboration. Clients are the experts on the content of their own stories, whereas counselors are experts on the process of change. So, the very first task of CCC is to initiate a relationship in which clients feel safe enough to narrate and reflect on their stories.

The relationship between client and counselor builds a secure base for a holding environment in which clients feel comfortable in communicating their ideas and life stories, including the "implicit unconscious" (Stern, (2004) or "unthought known" (Bollas, 1987). As E. M. Forster (1927/1985, p. 99) wrote, "How can I tell what I think til I see what I say?" Clients can more fully know and process implicit knowledge and unthought ideas as they tell their stories to counselors. In a secure relationship with a trusted counselor, clients are better able to understand and reflect on what they already know. For their part in the relationship, counselors trust that what clients need is already within them. Clients use counseling to make themselves more whole, more themselves by removing barriers that have blocked them from better knowing themselves and understanding their situations.

Reflection

Career construction and reconstruction evolve through explicit autobiographical reflection that deepens clients' knowledge of their own lives. CCC begins to focus self-reflection on the present sense of self because the past is always viewed from the present. Counselors move clients to examine the continuity and coherence in their lives by portraying clients' present self and situation as outcomes of their own choices and actions. This move in meaning-making positions clients to reorganize their life stories by viewing them from a different perspective.

During CCC the content for retrospective reflection comes from small stories elicited by scaffolding questions. The questions propel clients to create a space for reflection by stepping away from their problems. Then self-constructing and self-organizing processes occur as clients tell and reflect on initial stories that reveal their current understanding of contexts, circumstances, and challenges. This autobiographical reasoning about micro-narratives provides possibilities for sense-making and meaning construction. Telling the small stories enables clients to get outside of themselves and more readily examine their lives from a distance. Then they are able to reconstruct a macro-narrative with which to experience their lives within a larger story. Making sense within this larger story or revised identity leads to the conscious cultivation of intention.

Sense-making

Sense-making is a core element in CCC because it clarifies life purpose, fosters intentionality, and encourages commitmentf. Previous generations who lived in solid societies could commit themselves to an organization that would provide stability, a sense of purpose, and a framework for a 30-year career. Today, the liquid societies of post-modernity engender instability, uncertainty, and risk. In liquid societies, many people must answer for themselves the questions of "How shall I live?" and "How should I design my life to achieve my aspirations?" Social institutions no longer provide the normative scripts with which their parents and grandparents answered these questions. Today, individuals answer these questions by committing themselves to identity projects formed by self-authored intentions. This requires that individuals commit themselves to their own projects rather than to a career story already-written by an organization or institution.

CCC encourages clients to make sense of their lives by articulating purpose, forming intentions, and making commitments. Of course career decisions are made, yet the real outcome is a sense of purpose that informs the numerous choices that will compose a career. A sense of purpose begets intentionality that sets a direction in life. This is why CCC emphasizes sense-making to clarify the purpose that controls perception and illuminates possibilities. In short, purpose leads to intentions that steer action in the social world of work.

In CCC, sense-making involves constructing narratives. Clients enter counseling after they have completed a story, been de-storyed, or fallen out of story. They may no longer understand their situation and how to act in it. They must make sense of disorienting separations that have inter-rupted or disrupted life-as-usual. Most clients feel lost and believe that they are encountering novel situations without a script that tells them who they are and what to do. They need to interpret what is happening in order to compose a scenario for the next chapter in their stories. Making sense means they must understand the novel situation in words and stories that restore order and prompt adaptation. The new script plots a plausible account that clarifies what is occurring and poses possibilities for action. For career con-struction counselors, action denotes behavior infused with meaning. As Kelly (1955) long ago taught, people know the world by taking action and seeing what happens. Counsel-ing is completed when clients engage in deliberate actions to test the provisional understandings in the new narrative that they authored during counseling.

Career construction counselors engage in *sense-giving*, that is, an attempt to influence client *sense-making* and meaning construction by asking scaffolding questions that evoke personal stories. These story-crafting questions quickly lead to a new perspective from which to reconstruct and re-organize a novel account that prompts innovative action.

To respond to those counselors who worry that constructionist counseling requires them to interpret client meaning, I contend that sense-making differs from interpretation (Matlis & Christianson, 2014). Sense-making is the process by which people structure and give meaning to uncertain or ambiguous situations. Interpretation positions counselors as experts who identify latent content and reveal hidden meaning to prompt client insights. Interpretation implies that a frame of meaning already exists and counselors use clues to recognize it in clients. For example, in test interpretation counselors use clues from clients' behavior to place them in the RIASEC framework (Holland, 1997). In contrast, sense-making is concerned with client invention and discovery rather than counselor interpretation (Weick, 1995). In sense-making, clients first construct the events and perspectives that they themselves will then understand and think about by creating their own meaning framework, not using some pre-existing framework. In short, construction or authoring of a narrative precedes sense-making. It should also be noted that a client's preferred sense-making framework or perspective should not be considered as objective or correct. Any particular perspective is one among many possible organizations of experience that may be useful in making sense and generating meaning.

Chapter Two

Transition Narrative

Constructionist counselors use the first session to prompt clients to tell career stories and engage in autobiographical reflection and reasoning. Counselors devote the first session to eliciting a transition narrative and conducting a *Career Construction Interview*. During the second session, clients will use their responses to make sense of their transition, form intentions, set goals, and plan actions. To begin eliciting the transition narrative, counselors establish an initial connection with a client.

Eliciting the Transition Narrative

Goal

Create a working alliance by establishing a relationship, forming goals, and describing tasks (Bordin, 1979).

Rationale

In initiating the consultation, counselors orient clients to the process. They induct the client into counseling by explaining what to expect. They communicate implicitly or explicitly three aspects of the counseling process. First, clients are experts on the content of their own lives whereas counselors are experts on the process of change. Second, clients direct the counseling sessions, with counselors leading from behind by overseeing the process. And third, a counselor's job is to prompt clients to work. The genius of the counselor is in asking questions, not offering answers.

With this in mind, counselors meet clients where they are. Accepting clients' concerns and goals helps clients feel that they are the expert and are directing the session. Exploring clients' meaning for and feelings about their situation eases forward movement. In doing this, counselors recognize and reflect back the best in clients. Counselors also let clients know that they care. Clients consider indications of authentic caring to be incredibly moving. Many clients report that the most important moments occurred when their counselors showed that they cared.

Entry Question

After establishing an initial connection with clients and assuring confidentiality, counselors set the foundation for collaboration by asking the entry question. In providing academic advice or vocational guidance, counselors ask how they may be helpful because they are offering advice and guidance. Constructionist counselors prefer to ask, *How may I be useful to you?* In asking this entry question, constructionist counselors prefer the word "useful" because they want to learn how clients plan to use the consultation. After clients' initial response, counselors do not assume that they are finished. To open a client's mind to itself, counselors encourage clients to elaborate by asking, *Is there anything more?*

As clients speak, counselors listen for feelings. Some clients express emotions freely and fully whereas others seem stoic. Even if a client does not use feeling words, counselors attend to the felt meaning of the client's circumstances. With permission and prompting, clients may talk about deeper emotions that suggest the cutting edge of change. Negative and moderately intense emotions signal the need for change and provide energy to fuel sense-making. Some counselors explain to clients that emotions are "communication from I to me" (Leitner & Fraidley, 2003) that direct attention to what one might become.

It is a good idea to normalize a client's problem by explaining that the problem is understandable and experienced by many people. The explanation should state a clear conceptualization of the client's situation and foreshadow new ways of thinking about it. Counselors do this briefly unless a client expresses guilt or shame, that is, has a problem about the problem. In this case, counselors process the client's feelings about having the problem.

Counselors differ in how much background information they collect. Personally, I collect very little backstory because I believe the relevant information will emerge as needed during counseling. However, some counselors prefer to learn more details about clients' educational and vocational past. They may spend a considerable amount of time taking a history; yet this usually makes the counselor more comfortable not the client. It also begins the session with the counselor controlling the proceedings and may even suggest to the client that the counselor is similar to a physician who collects information, makes a diagnosis, and then resolves the problem.

Tips

Convey confidence that the intervention will be useful.

Acknowledge and compliment any specific actions that a client has already taken to address the career problem.

Validate protests about and critiques of the problem or those who support it, including the client herself or himself.

Use metaphors that resonate with the client's metaphors. For example, if a client feels lost at sea, then the counselor uses kindred metaphors such as compass, navigation, storm, and safe harbor.

Consider gaps in the story, that is, what is not said or cannot be said.

When clients cry they are feeling what they need.

Acknowledge the tears and follow them to the unmet needs.

Respect client silence. Wait for the next need or figure to arise from the grounded self. The power of a pause lies in this fertile void.

Explore sighs by getting full expression of whatever clients say next. The sigh may have been caused by a thought that took their breath away.

Counter generalizations such as *everyone feels that way.*

Contest sentences that state *should, ought,* or *must* by suggesting instead *could, prefer,* or *want.*

Reinforce words that signal need such as *hope, seek, desire, miss,* and *lack.*

Notice for later discussion booster words that intensify meaning because they may signal rigid behavior or potential stressors: *very, extremely, always, really, totally,* and *absolutely.*

Stick with what the client wants, not interventions and procedures that you enjoy or think the client needs. You may recommend additional interventions or services at the conclusion of career counseling.

Assessing Narrative Content and Form

Individuals seek counseling to make sense of issues and cope with events that are novel, ambiguous, or unexpected. Clients' responses to the entry question tell the story with which they hold their current transition. This story provides a frame for the ensuing consultation. Counselors assess how well a client stories the problem, that is, makes sense of the experience and wraps it up in a story. Counselors understand the short story, which I call the *transition narrative*, by looking forward to its potential unfolding into thematic concerns that it foreshadows. The transition narrative beckons counselors forward by foreseeing complications, promising new insights, and suggesting possible resolutions. Experienced counselors often foresee the outcome of counseling from the inchoate vista of this short story. However, the client does not yet envision those outcomes and needs to experience the process of counseling to understand what they have foretold in their transition narrative.

Narration Content

To begin to understand a client's story, counselors appraise both the story content and how clients tell the story in terms of meaning and feeling. The story content describes how the client positions self in relation to the problem, other people, and the counselor (Madill, Sermpezis & Barkham, 2005). Four questions guide the counselors' appraisal of story content.

> With regard to the problem, does the client describe the situation in fixed terms using negative labels and psychological terms or more flexibly with a few positive emotions?

> With regard to self, does the client express a sense of personal agency to cope with the problem?

> With regard to other people, does the client position self as having social support and instrumental resources?

> With regard to the counselor, does the client position self as an active collaborator?

Counselors begin almost immediately to move clients to the position of an agent who will resolve the problem in collaboration with the counselor and by using community resources.

Narrating process

In addition to story content, counselors assess how clients tell their stories. Constructionist counselors consider how to best begin to join the client by assessing the meaning and feeling in the narrative content. Counselors ask themselves, *How clearly and coherently does the story content express what it means and how it feels to the client?* The creators of emotion-focused therapy, have identified six different ways in which clients may shape a story (Angus & Greenberg, 2011). These story forms readily apply to the transition narratives that clients tell about what they want to accomplish through counseling. Some story forms lead counselors to concentrate on understanding the meaning of the content while other story forms draw attention to feelings. The six story forms are the same old story, untold story, unstoryed emotions, changing story, empty story, and conflict story.

Same old story in which a client presents a generalized representation of the situation or problem. Marker words include *never, always, constantly,* and *forever.*

Example: *I am trying to figure out if I should remain in my current job or not. I have always done this job since I got out of the military. I want to know if I should stay in this field. I have thought about changing jobs many times over the years. But I never did. I always decided that I would remain where I am at until I retire. But now I am again thinking a lot about changing jobs. I think about it constantly.*

When counselors wonder what a client's story means, they encourage clients to specify its meaning by elaborating their stories with more details and particulars (Kashdam,

Barrett, & McKnight, 2015). To help clients who tell the same old story, counselors prompt clients to move from generalizations and clichés by elaborating the unique content of their stories and then consider the meaning of this content and the feelings aroused by the meaning.

Untold story in which a client dissembles or omits a significant element from the narrative.

Example: *A first-year medical student stated that entering the medical school building depresses him. When asked about his parents' aspirations for him, he stated that they do not care what he does for a living. They only want him to be happy. During the second session, when the counselor was puzzled about the client's situation, the client revealed that his mother had put tremendous pressure on him to become a physician and he does not want to do so.*

To help clients who omit important elements of their stories, counselors may ask clients about something that from the counselor's understanding of the story is absent yet implicit. However, sometimes counselors must wait until clients feel more comfortable elaborating their stories.

Unstoryed emotions in which a client's narrative expresses strong feeling without an obvious cause. The feelings lack context and personal meaning.

Example: *Currently I am in the process of beginning to transition out of my graduate program. I have not given a lot of thought to my future career profession and life after college. I am extremely nervous about entering into the real world. Now it is time to step out and actually be a professional and take on a full-time job. I definitely know what I want to do and I have three job opportunities. But I am scared to leave college so I am thinking of going for a doctorate so I can stay on campus where I am safe.*

Counselors curious about the presence of strong feelings absent meaning usually use active listening and empathic responding (Carkhuff, 1969). With strong emotions, counselors attempt to understand the meaning that fuels the feelings.

Changing story in which emergent meaning signals that a client may be in the process of transforming or changing. The narrative may include phrases such as "I just recalled" or "I am not sure this is important but..."

Example: *I am graduating in four weeks and I thought I knew what I wanted to do. All of sudden I do not know if I want to do it, especially for the rest of my life. I have found a new field that I am very interested in but do not know if I am qualified for it or need more training.*

As stories change, counselors may try to establish a line of continuity from past through present into the future by inquiring about the problem's background, that is, other elements that underlie the situation existing at the beginning of the main narrative.

Empty story in which a client tells a dramatic story that focuses on external events without any feeling.

Example: *My boss is sexually harassing me and I need to find a new job. I am not sure what I want to do. Maybe I should take this opportunity to change fields. This would give me a fresh start.*

With a story lacking feelings, counselors try to determine if the client is trying to avoid anxiety and tension. With these clients, counselors move sensitively and slowly into feelings by establishing a secure basis for client trust and building a holding environment to contain the pain. They then help clients to identify emotions by having them notice non-verbal expressive cues, such as clenching the jaw or gripping the chair. In response, counselors choose words carefully to more fully form vague emotional expressions.

Conflict story in which a client is perplexed by feelings or goals that conflict with each other. For example, their goal may conflict with a parent's goals for them or their own goals of being altruistic and affluent may clash.

Example: *I am looking for a clearer picture of what the next step is for me. The picture is unfocused because it intermixes with my family. I think I know what I want to do but it may not be the right choice for my family. It might affect them negatively. If I focus on my career the picture is clear; if I focus on my family the picture is clear but different. When I try to focus on both my career and family at the same time, the picture is hazy.*

The better the explanation of meaning and the greater the awareness of feelings, the less likely that a client will be overwhelmed. Clear meaning and evident feelings inform counselors about how to join the client. Regardless of the transitional narrative's form, to propel problem solving and goal setting counselors eventually must use empathic responses to help clients explore their present feelings as well as discuss the unmet needs and unstated meanings that prompt these emotions. Accessing more emotions improves coping because two emotions are better than one (Kashdan, Barrett, & McKnight, 2015). Labeled emotions that are tailored to the situation are easier to regulate, and they either facilitate a person's strivings or become irrelevant.

Counselors may assess clients' feelings about their situation by considering the emotional vocabulary in the transition narrative. The following questions may be helpful in this regard.

How many feeling words does the client use?

How many different feeling words are used?

How specific are the feeling words?

Does the client show awareness of complexity by using both positive and negative feeling words?

Does the client recognize her or his own feelings?

Does the client use these emotions to just express unpleasant experience or to fuel a desire to act?

With quick answers to these questions, counselors are ready to respond fully to a client's transition narrative.

Co-Constructing Counseling Goals

Having heard the client's presenting concerns and maybe some backstory, counselors then consider what the client seeks from counseling. Counselors privilege clients' experience as they explore what a client does and does not want. They need to recognize clients' assumptions about how counseling works. Counselors emphasize to clients that they must speak up when the counselor misunderstands something, not defer to the counselor as a professional. Some counselors even ask, *As your counselor, what would be the worst thing I could do?* Counselors also explain how clients are the expert on their own experience and that the counselor is just trying to get close to it.

The counselor is now ready to co-construct shared goals for counseling. As Abraham Lincoln once noted, "a goal well-set is half achieved." Counselors work to clarify the client's stated goals in a manner designed to increase client self-awareness and further what a client is trying to do. During this discussion counselors remain alert to client signals about additional goals or implied concerns. Together, client and counselor formulate the problem and state explicit goals for counseling. Counselors are sure to write the goals on a sheet of paper because when terminating counseling they will confirm that the client has achieved those goals.

In setting goals, counselors must believe that the outcomes can be accomplished. For example, as a career construction counselor I have met clients who request help in writing a resumé. Before going any further, I refer them to a placement specialist. If counselors refer them at the end of the session or the beginning of the next session, clients may conclude that the counselor does not like working with them.

Having reached a consensus on goals, counselors create a context for conversation by describing boundaries and confidentiality. To foster collaboration, counselors specify what they will   expect of the client and what the client may expect from them. To do this, counselors briefly describe the tasks for each session and the rationale for the procedures that they will use. This description demystifies the process by making it transparent. To learn more in regards to opening an interview, read about designing projects for career construction (Savickas, 2015b); the importance of the first exchange (Stiles, Leiman, Shapiro, Hardy, Barkham, Detert, & Llewelyn, 2006); and positioning the client (Madill, Sermpezis, & Barkham, 2005).

Having created a working alliance by establishing a relationship, setting goals, and describing tasks, the counselor is ready to conduct a Career Construction Interview.

Chapter Three

Career Construction Interview

The Career Construction Interview (CCI) is a structured dialogue during which counselors inquire about five topics that uncover life themes and inform decision making about the current transition. The topics address role models; magazines, television programs, or websites; current favorite story; frequent saying or motto; and early recollections. Counselors begin the interview after establishing a relationship, aligning goals, and describing the counseling process. Counselors then ask the five CCI questions to provide a scaffold for making sense, declaring purpose, forming intentions, and prompting action.

The CCI concentrates client reflection through a gentle, progressive, and step-by-step inquiry that leads them to deeper accounts of their past experience and current concerns. As clients respond to the questions, counselors show interest and curiosity. Counselors also try to elicit novel ideas and elaborate client statements that express increased motivation for dealing with barriers, changes accomplished and anticipated, heightened self-awareness, reconsideration of problem causes and consequences, new perspectives on the problem, deeper understandings of the problem, and intentions to explore and plan.

CCI Question 1: Role Models

Goal

Identify nouns and adjectives that describe a client's construction and conception of self.

Rationale

Career construction counselors inquire about role models because selecting role models is the very first career choice that individuals make. If a counselor can ask only one question, then this is it. Answers to this question provide the characters and attributes that the client used as a blueprint for self-construction. During late adolescence, individuals integrate these attributes or identity fragments into an initial vocational identity.

Question

Who did you admire when you were growing up? Who were your heroes/heroines? I am interested in learning about three people, other than your mother and father, who you admired when you were about six to nine years old. They can be real people you knew or didn't know personally, make-believe people like super-heroes and cartoon characters, or characters in books or the media.

After a client names a role model, counselors then say, *I always ask for three role models, so please tell me two more.*

Having obtained three role models, counselors then have clients describe each one in turn. If a client merely describes what a role model did, then counselors ask for personality traits: *I want to know what the model was like as a person. Please give some personality characteristics or descriptions.* Also, if a client uses mostly descriptors that are concrete in terms of physical attributes, then counselors press for words that are more abstract in terms of internal psychological states such as thinking, feeling, and valuing. Counselors press until the client produces some adjectives and nouns that describe the model's psychological make-up. They are sure to get at least four characteristics for each role model. Also, they listen for repeated words   because repetition signals core attributes.

Tips

After collecting adjectives that describe the three role models, you may have what you need. However, if you want more descriptors, then ask the following.

>*How are you like .....?*
>*How are you different from .....?*
>*What do the three role models have in common?*
>*How do the role models differ from each other?*

If a client responds that mother or father was a role model, then counselors ask for someone else. Parents are taken in as heteronomous <u>influences,</u> in comparison to role models who are taken on as autonomous <u>identifications.</u> Other family members may be considered to be role models-- including grandparents, aunts, uncles, and cousins.

After completing the inquiry about three role models, counselors may return to ask about the parents, out of respect for the client having mentioned them. Usually, I ask a simple question from attachment research: *Give me three words that describe your mother.* Then I ask for three words for father. Occasionally, if suggested by the transition narrative, I ask for a fuller description of parents.

If after trying, a client cannot think of any role models from early childhood, counselors may ask about role models from middle childhood or even early adolescence.

CCI Question 2: Magazines, Television, Websites

Goal

Identify the types of environments, activities, and objects that interest the client.

Rationale

Interest is the feeling experienced when one's attention, concern, or curiosity is particularly engaged by something. Interest assessment may be done in three main ways: inventoried such as with the *Strong Interest Inventory*, expressed such as with occupational daydreams in the *Self-Directed Search*, and manifest such as demonstrated in activities. The preferred method when counseling an individual is to assess manifest interests, because they have the best predictive validity. Of course, interest inventories are the preferred method when doing group vocational guidance because counselors cannot interview each member of the group.

Counselors assess manifest interests by identifying characteristics of the actual environments in which clients routinely place themselves, either actually or vicariously. This is because interest involves a psychosocial connection between a person and an environment. Therefore, interests always require an object or environment. Accordingly, counselors inquire about the environments that draw clients' interest. This is CCC's method for examining client's occupational resemblance, congruence, and correspondence. Constructionist do not ordinarily use interest inventories. However, some counselors new to CCC continue to use inventories to survey interests until they become confident in their own ability to assess manifest interests. If a counselor prefers to inventory interests with a commercial product, then the results fit here.

Question

Counselors usually begin to assess manifest interests by inquiring about magazines: *Do you subscribe to or regularly read any magazines?* After counselors have elicited three favorite magazines, they interrogate each one to uncover a client's interests. They may say, *Please tell me what the magazine's stories are about.* If they ask follow-up questions, they use motivational language.

"What attracts you to ...?"
"How do you find ... interesting?"
"What appeals to you in ...?"
"Why do you prefer ...?"
"What do you like about the magazine?"

Many people today do not read magazines. If a client has no favorite magazines or the counselor seeks more information about interests, then counselors ask about television programs. *"Are there any television shows that you watch regularly?" Is any television show appointment TV for you?"* As usual, counselors ask for three examples. Counselors then interrogate television programs with the same motivational questions used for magazines.

A few clients neither read magazines nor watch television; or if they do, they do not have any favorites. In this case, counselors ask for favorite websites: *Which internet websites do your visit regularly?* A follow-up question about websites can be *Do you view Reddit?* This popular website presents a network of communities based on the viewer's interests. Another technology-related question may inquire about favorite computer games. Again, counselors ask for three sites and interrogate each one.

Tips

The goal is not to survey or inventory shows or reading materials, it to determine the type of vicarious environments an individual prefers.

If more information is needed beyond vicarious environments, then counselors may ask about leisure activities.

Make sure to identify the actual interests that prompt preferences for magazines, television programs, websites, or games.

Have clients explain in their own words what attracts them to the activities or objects. If a counselor watches the same television show, she or he may think that they know what attracts the client's interests but it is absolutely necessary to hear the client's explanation because it may differ from what attracts the counselor to the program.

CCI Question 3: Favorite Story

Goal

Understand the stories or cultural scripts that a client may be using to envision the transition outcome.

Rationale

A story from a movie or a book becomes a favorite for individuals because it depicts a strategy that they need in scripting their transition. Implicit in the favorite story may be an incipient plan for the next episode in their life story. Clients' favorite stories lay open their lives to themselves and clarify what they might do next. In clients' favorite stories, counselors typically see a faint outline of what clients think may be possible or even an inchoate plan.

An individual's character as an actor remains fairly stable during a life-time, whereas scripts change to enable an actor to adapt to a new work setting. Each new setting may need a new script; thus individuals typically use a new story to make a career change. A new favorite story provides viable schemes and strategies from which to script a scenario for the career transition. Also, a new life stage may require a new script. For example, a script useful during emerging adulthood may be unsuitable during retirement. Looking back over your life, you may be able to identify a favorite story from childhood, a different one from adolescence, and still another one during emerging adulthood. Counselors usually find that an individual's scripts from different life periods show some similarity because they repeat overarching themes that provide continuity in life stories. Occasionally counselors meet clients who, beginning in childhood, maintain a single favorite story over several decades. Although the basic story remains the same, these clients usually gain new insights with which they revise and adapt the script to cope with the demands of new work settings and life stages. In addition to changes in settings and stages, different life roles require different scripts. For example the life role of intimate partner may require a different script than does the work role. That is why individuals perform multiple identities, an identity being a self-in-a-role. Counselors may address, as pertinent, construction and reconstruction of relationship roles along with work roles.

Question

Currently, what is your favorite story from a book or movie? Tell me the story. Most clients choose a story from a book or a movie. However, clients may report a favorite story from a rock opera such as Quadraphenia, a comic book such as Batman: The Dark Knight Returns, the Bible such as Sampson and Delilah, a graphic novel such as Blankets, or a children's book such as The Little Train That Could.

Tips

In asking the question, emphasize "currently" or "right now." Career construction theory views scripts as sources of adaptability and flexibility in new settings or stages. Asking for a client's "all-time" favorite movie may access an overarching theme rather than a current scheme.

Be sure to have clients tell the story in their own words. They should use at least four or five sentences, otherwise their narrative may omit a key element of the script.

If the story does not make immediate sense in relation to

the transition narrative, then ask for a second favorite story. Later when you have time, you probably will be able to understand the place of both stories in the client's macro-narrative.

CCI Question 4: Favorite Saying

Goal

Learn the advice that a client has been giving to self.

Rationale

A CCC goal is to have clients hear and respect their own wisdom. This goal follows from the principle that "the patient and only the patient has the answers" (Winnicott, 1969). A favorite saying articulates the best advice that a client has for herself or himself. The advice typically bears directly on the problem described in the transition narrative and usually makes immediate sense to both the client and counselor. The saying conveys an auto-therapy in which clients repeatedly tell the self what they must do to advance their story to a new chapter and in so doing become more complete. The counselor reiterates and reinforces this advice in later discussions with the client.

Question

What is your favorite saying or motto? If after a while and a few more prompts a client cannot think of one then counselors may ask, *Have you seen any saying that you like on a poster or a car bumper sticker?* And if needed, *Do you have any saying you think of frequently?*

Tips

If a client cannot think of a favorite saying, then ask, *Would you be willing to make one up now?* For example, a 14 year-old girl who wanted to become a novelist created *Make a wish, take a chance, and watch your dreams come true.*

If a client's saying does not make immediate sense to you, then ask for a second saying.

If you notice a tattoo, ask its meaning. It may depict a symbolic tenet that guides behavior.

CCI Question 5: Early Recollections

Goal

Understand the perspective from which a client views the problem presented in the transition narrative.

Rationale

It is useful for counselors to consider the perspective from which clients view the presenting problem or current career concern. To explore a client's perspective, constructionist counselors inquire about early recollections because these memories usually portray a highly personal reconstruction of experience that represents the current situation (Mayman, 1960; Mosak, 1958). Typically, the first ER alludes to the perspective from which the client views the career problem. Continuing to use the metaphor of a self performing on a stage, the ERs tell how the director of the play sees the scene.

Question

What are your earliest recollections? I am interested in hearing three stories about things that happened to you when you were three to six years old. When a client is finished communicating each ER counselors ask, *If you were to assign a feeling to that memory, what feeling would it be?* After writing down that overall feeling, counselors ask a second question, *If you had a photograph of the most vivid part of that memory, what would it show?* After collecting the three ERs, counselors work with clients to compose a headline for each ER. Counselors say to the client, *Please give me a headline for each memory. The headline is like that used for a story in a newspaper or a title for a movie. A good headline has a verb in it.* Then counselors read aloud the first ER and wait for the client to compose a headline. The process has clients author their own meaning and feel its emotional truth. Counselors work with a client until the client thinks the headline is just right. Assigning titles to ERs is not simply a linguistic activity; it is an expression of authority in which clients themselves make sense of their experiences.

Tips

The ER must be about a specific incident. For example, if a client said *Every Sunday we visited Grandmother*, then counselors would ask for a story about a particular time when she or he visited Grandmother.

Try to get at least four sentences for each ER.

Be sure to get a verb in each headline as well as a feeling word for each ER.

Closing the Career Construction Interview

After completing the CCI, counselors signal the end of the first session by asking clients if there is anything else that they want to mention. Counselors preview that next session by explaining to clients that during this first session they acted as a biographer or journalist trying to learn the client's story. Counselors inform clients that before the next session, they will study the collection of small stories and compose them into a large story to use in the client's decision making and planning. Then, counselors schedule an appointment for a week later.

Chapter Four

Reconstructing a Life Portrait

Between sessions, counselors combine the small stories into a large story or life portrait that unfolds deeper meaning and fosters decision making.

Plot and Theme

Goal

Emplot clients' small stories into a large story that changes perspective, improves self-understanding, clarifies what is at stake in the transition, eases decision making, and prompts action.

Rationale

Counselors structure the collage of small stories from the Career Construction Interview to emplot a life portrait. They seek to foster client transformation by reconstructing a client's small stories in fresh and figurative terms that transcend the obvious. This re-authoring enables clients to invest the transition narrative with some restorative meaning for their ongoing lives. Dramatic re-engagement with their own life history opens options for clients to more fully inhabit their lives as they step into the future.

In reconstructing a client's stories, counselors do not revise the small stories, rather they apply a structure to emplot the several small stories into one large story. Small stories tell of actual events, whereas the plot refers to the story line. Simply stated, in CCC, the plot is the counselor's particular arrangement of events into a larger story. The same story can be told using a variety of plot lines or arrangement of events. Counselors devise ways of construing a plot for clients' experiences that is useful in the current transition. They do not know the truth or what the stories really mean. Counselors' arrangement of a plot is neither uniquely objective nor idiosyncratically subjective. Instead, plots reconstruct a large story that highlights values and gives new meaning to the small stories.

Among the many possible organizations of experience that may be useful in generating a sense of meaning and surfacing values, constructionist counselors use a generic plot structure to reconstruct a large story. To arrange client micro-narratives into this general plot, counselors use the pattern-recognition schema embedded in the deep-plot structure of the CCI questions. The scaffolding questions have been sequenced to link clients' micro-narratives into a macro-narrative. The five story-crafting questions inquire about *self*, *stage* on which to perform the self, *script* for the next act, a *dvice* on how to begin, and a basic *perspective* on the transition.

Using the general storyline to sequentially emplot a client's micro-narratives into a macro-narrative is uncomplicated and easy to understand. What takes a little more practice is recognizing a theme that runs through the plot. A career theme is the main idea or issue that unifies the occupational plot. In distilling a theme that runs through the storyline, counselors select from multiple explanatory possibilities, usually choosing the one that provides the most continuity and coherence in unifying the plot. The chosen theme must be accurate enough to contain new understandings about the past and present as well as prompt future action. Following the general plot structure for CCC, counselors condense the most important aspects of the small stories around the chosen theme. In so doing, counselors emphasize the essential meaning of the theme for the current transition. In reconstructing a macro-narrative, counselors repeatedly refer to and reinforce the theme by discussing its manifestation in the beliefs, values, and goals expressed in client micro-narratives.

Retelling a client's stories following a theme in the generic sequence does not imply interpreting the stories; rather, it aims to integrate them into a broader sense of significance that deepens meaning and suggests how to extend the story in life-affirming ways. As appropriate and relevant for particular clients, this involves discussing what is vital to them, what they need to express, the sacrifices they might make, and the balance they must restore.

Tips

What happened in the client's first telling must remain pretty much the same in the counselor's retelling.

Be concise. Clients do not need all the information originally presented.

Animate the story by using small words and present-tense verbs.

Do not judge, analyze, or explain. Just organize using phrases from the client's responses to the scaffolding questions.

Task 1. Frame the Perspective

Use early recollection to help clients comprehend and evaluate their analogies for the transition problem and to concentrate attention on issues they cannot ignore.

Begin by completing the first sentence in the life portrait: *In facing this transition, my underlying concern has reminded me* .... This sentence may eventually stand alone as a single sentence or serve as the topic sentence for a paragraph.

Rationale

The last question in the CCI seeks information about a

client's perspective on the transition by asking for early recollections. The question is last in the CCI sequence because it is the most personal. Thus, counselors ask it only after having established a trustworthy relationship, one in which the client has formed some attachment to the counselor. Because it is usually deeply meaningful, composing the portrait starts with the perspective taken in the ERs.

At the first level of meaning, counselors consider how the early recollections, particularly the first one, provide a perspective from which to view the problem presented in the transition narrative. Counselors consider how viewing the problem from the perspective of the ER illuminates a way forward. They may even draw an analogy between the ERs and the transition narrative if they seem to share some similar characteristics. For example, a client thinking about changing jobs described her ER as looking out her bedroom window trying to see what was happening outside. She wanted to leave her job yet was hesitant to look into her options because she felt safe in her current position.

At a second and deeper level, counselors consider whether the perspective is also a preoccupation, one that may be turned into an occupation. Rather than only a perspective on the current issue, a preoccupation may be used as a cognitive schema for interpreting many diverse experiences. At this level, ERs often reveal an important core role or unmet need.

At the third and deepest level, counselors consider whether an intense pain anchors the preoccupation. Pain is not an emotion; it is a holistic system response to trauma and wound. Pain arises from being excluded from or losing something highly valued. Metaphorically, the wound may also be a womb from which something new is produced. As the 13th century Persian poet Rumi wrote, "The wound is where the light enters you." The light typically illuminates an alternative story, a way forward that is implicit in the pain. Counselors may follow the pain into the womb to identify unmet needs and find what is being formed. Counselors remain empathically connected to clients as they increase self-awareness of their needs and how to meet them. Most clients feel what they need, so tears often accompany increased self-awareness.

Some beginning counselors may be uncomfortable sitting with the pain as clients descend into their wound. These counselors may skip the ER question. They may work from the solution portrayed in role models without directly witnessing the pain. However, when counselors feel secure in holding clients' pain and possibilities they consider whether the transition reactivates a rupture in attachment or spins the client's world off its axis. In working at this level, counselors are doing therapy or healing. At its deepest level, pain puts the current issue into new perspective by relating it to a backstory, and eventually returns attention to repositioning the perspective described previously as the first level of meaning.

Assess

Although the content off ERs comes from the past, the stories are about the present. They are part of forming in the present a viable vision and strategy for the future. Memory is actively selective; and clients intuitively choose early recollections that pertain to the presenting problem. For example, consider a client having difficulty at work. She tells an ER about a babysitter locking her outside of the house when she was three years old. The counselor needs to understand how today the client feels she is being locked out of opportunities at her workplace. Or consider a client who tells an ER of having his diaper changed when he did not want it done. The counselor may wonder about the unwanted changes occurring in the client's career right now. Notice that the main verb in these two ERs carries the meaning, as it does in most ERs. Counselors need to amplify these verbs in the life portrait. Especially consider if the main verb in the first ER expresses or resembles the movement or lack of movement that a client depicts in formulating the career problem. If so, the counselor may have the client consider whether that way of moving could be reoccurring as the client faces the current career problem.

In addition to believing that ERs are really about the present, constructionist counselors know that clients tell the stories that they themselves need to hear. From all their possible stories, clients select those stories that support current goals and inspire action. Rather than remembering, they re-member the past so that prior events support current choices and lay a groundwork for the future. The counselor's task is to urge clients to hear the message *from-the-self-to-the-self* that each ER contains.

Counselors may make sense of ERs by using an impressionistic and intuitive approach. Alternatively, they may use one of numerous interpretive systems. I recommend the method described by Clark (2002). Personally, I try to make sense of ERs by combining intuition with a succinct, logical framework. I start with a general impression of how the client relates to other people in the story. Then I consider and amplify the first verb because it often indicates a person's most frequent way of moving in the world. The feeling word is probably an emotion felt often, particularly during a transition. The headline usually clarifies the main meaning of the memory and suggests a theme. Finally, I compare the ERs to the problem presented in the transition narrative. In doing so, I consider the possibility that a goal for the transition is to actively master the problem in the ER. For example, if people are locked out they must find a way back in or move to another place. If people are forced to change, they must find a way to maintain some continuity in their lives.

Example. A 35 year old woman, herein referred to as W.W., sought career counseling to consider her career options when her son enters the first grade. Her ER follows.

> *I remember at age three or four being in the hospital in my bed which had bars all around it. Up around it. The lights were low, the room was dark. I was waiting for my Mom to come to the hospital to sit with me. I got upset because I felt she was not going to show up. Time could not move fast enough. I remember that they gave me a 7 UP or Sprite while I was waiting. Finally she showed up and had a goose for me. It was Mother Goose.*

Interpersonal orientation: Wants relationships

First verb: Waiting (she wants, hopes, dreams)

Feeling: Alone, upset, isolated

Headline: Where is my Mom?

Perspective: Being separated from other people and feeling alone. Wants to connect with other people.

Passive to active: Help people who are alone and need nurturance.

> W.W.'s life portrait sentence 1: *In facing this transition, my underlying concern has reminded me that I fear being alone and abandoned.*

Story Sequence Analysis

It is a good practice to ask clients for three early recollections because clients often elaborate their perspective from different vantage points in a set of stories. I follow a client's thoughts from ER to ER by applying the principles of story sequence analysis devised by Arnold (1962). The first early recollection announces the issue that most concerns a client. The ER usually indicates how clients are stuck or suffering. They may be trapped in this story because it is a boundary experience. Buhler (1935, p. 58) referred to *boundary experiences* as something an individual feels as the edge of self beyond which they cannot move. The second ER often intensifies that concern by elaborating it. Things get worse before they get better. The third ER frequently presents a potential solution or resolution. Counselors inspect the third ER for a transformational activity through which clients may begin to turn passive suffering into active mastery. The transformational ER absorbs the pain; a client is less pushed by pain and more pulled by possibilities.

Consider the following example. A client reported his first ER as, *I remember moving to a new house.* I amplified the first verb, thinking that it represented a frequent action in his life as well as a perspective on his current career concern. I used my intuition to imagine him as moving, enjoying movement, liking to be on the move, being a mover and shaker, being moved, having motivation, and hating being immobile. I also realized that the move he described was to a new house. Thus, moving to new situations is an important element in the career theme, probably with both positive and negative elements. In the second ER, he recalled his difficulty in adjusting to the move. *One day I was riding my bike up the driveway, peddling as fast as I could to avoid being sucked downhill into a morass of trouble.* These two ERs re-presented his career problem of having just moved to yet another new job and working as hard as he could yet having trouble establishing himself. He felt that forces beyond his control were pulling him down. I wrote this life-portrait sentence for him to consider: *In facing this transition, my underlying concern has reminded me that I fear being sucked into a morass of trouble when I move to something new.*

His third ER pointed to a potential solution. In that recollection, he was four years old when his mother bought him several birthday cards. As she read them to him, he was amazed that you could put speech on paper and understand it. He said, *I think that this filled me with a sense of wonder.* Maybe words on paper can solve the problem of being pulled down. Having spent his career moving in and out of more than eight positions in the same occupation, at age 55 he sought consultation about an occupational change. He was financially secure and wanted to pursue something new, such as running for political office. Quickly, it became apparent that the something new was becoming an author and motivational speaker. His specialty would be teaching people how to adjust to new situations without being sucked into a morass.

To get started, try linking a client's three headlines to determine if they compose a longer story. They are usually in order from first to third, yet sometimes the order may be from third to first. Write the headline from the first ER and then a sentence or two that observes the perspective and feelings that it portrays. Be sure to amplify the most important verb in the ER, usually it is the first one. Then write the second headline and add a sentence or two to explain how it elaborates the first ER. Finally, write the third headline and a few sentences about how it may suggest resolving the problem. Here is an example of following a client's thoughts from ER to ER.

Your first headline read, "Girl Tired of the Same Old Story." You feel bored and frustrated with repetitive tasks and experiences. But in your second headline you explain that "Girl Fears Change." You seem anxious about changing from the secure position that you have established despite it being maddeningly boring. In your third headline you say that "Girl Takes a New Perspective." You explain that you have to change the way you see things in order to change the way you do things. Looking from a new perspective is intriguing, challenging, dramatic, and engaging.

When reading a story-sequence analysis to clients, counselors have clients reflect upon and comment in turn on each headline and its explanation and then again at the end of the third headline as a way of tracing the progression.

Tips

Prompt self-reflection and empower clients by using insight words such as *think, realize,* and *believe* as well as causal words such as *because, effect,* and *reason.*

Pause to process feelings evoked by the discussion.

Use a compelling metaphor when calling something new into existence. Metaphors can help clients move from the known into the unknown. The ERs offer a rich source of metaphors that have the advantage of being generated by clients, thus being particularly meaningful to them. For example, in an ER a client described how walking down stairs backwards gave her a new perspective. We then used that metaphor to discuss how she might need to step down the career ladder to take a new perspective before making a major transition.

Task 2. Describe the Self

At this point, counselors try to get a glimpse of clients' self-conceptions through the meanings that they have created.

Complete a second sentence for the life portrait: *I am* _____, _____, _____, *and* _____.

Rationale

Role models are imaginative resources that individuals use to develop their personal characteristics. The choice of role models indicates decisions about self-construction and the characteristics that individuals believe they need to develop. Clients' descriptions of role-model attributes reveal their core conceptions of themselves. The words that clients use to describe their role models apply equally to themselves. During adolescence individuals coalesce the attributes that they imitated into a coherent identity. Counselors amalgamate these same attributes into a verbal sketch that portrays a brief, general account of a client's character. The sketch is not a summing up but a synthesis (Erikson, 1968), a configuration that reconciles and integrates multiple personal characteristics.

Assess

In sketching the contours of a character, counselors identify core self-conceptions based on primacy, repetition, and complexity. They begin by concentrating on the first noun or adjective that a client used to describe the first role model. Primacy usually signals importance. Similar to the first verb in the first early recollection, the first attribute in a role-model description identifies a core characteristic.

In addition to primacy, frequency also indicates importance. Following the psycho-lexical hypothesis, counselors scrutinize repeated words and phrases because words used more often describe more salient features of self. Also, repeated words refer to stable attributes that pertain to more consistent behavior over a wider range of situations (Leising, Scharloth, Lohse, & Wood, 2014).

In addition to repeated words, counselors also ascertain the total number of unique attributes because it indicates complexity of the self-concept.

Finally, counselors evaluate whether two words suggest conflicting characteristics and if an apparent contradiction is resolved in a coherent synthesis. Concentrating on two characteristics that ordinarily do not go together usually leads to deeper understanding of the client. For example, a client may use both tough and tender to describe self. These adjectives usually do not go together yet the client has incorporated them both, maybe in protecting weaker individuals from bullies. Learning how the client integrated the opposing attributes highlights some unique feature of a clients' self-construction.

Having a set of self-relevant descriptors, counselors formulate a brief and sharply drawn characterization of the client. For example, W.W. who recalled waiting for her mother to arrive at the hospital said her first role model as a child had been Wonder Women. She described Wonder Women, and implicitly herself, with the words *helpful, strong but not violent, and always there to save the day.* She described her second model, Xenia, *as strong, not afraid, protected innocence, stood up for others, fought for what she believed.* Her third model was Barney who she described as *optimistic, caring, and always helping others.*

W.W.'s life-portrait sentence 2: *I am strong, caring, and helpful. I always protect the innocent but not in a violent way.*

Notice that W.W. twice used the booster word "always."

The counselor will in due course discuss the potential stress caused by believing that one must always offer help to other people.

Tips

Ignore purely evaluative words such as *good*, *great*, and *bad*.

More abstract words refer to more influential attributes in a self-concept hierarchy. When clients use several similar words to describe their role models, chose the most repeated word or the word at the highest level of abstraction that still describes the behavior. For example, choose kind from among a group of similar descriptors such as charitable, considerate, courteous, or thoughtful.

If describing a role model evokes emotions, explore what the role model symbolizes in terms of meaning and feeling.

Internalization of parents and role models play different roles in the psyche. Individuals choose their role models, not their parents. Clients *take in* their parental influences but *take on* their role-model identifications.

In collectivist cultures, the influence of parental guiding lines plays a stronger role in career construction than does identification with role models.

Task 3. Link ERs to Role Model Attributes

Trace the path from the perspective and preoccupations in ERs to solutions presented in the form of attributes engendered by role models.

Arc the client's character in completing a third sentence for the life portrait, one that usually is a topic sentence for a full paragraph: *To solve problems in growing up, I turned _____ into _____.*

Rationale

Clients change as they find in their role models solutions to their problems. A life portrait portrays the characteristics that a client copied from role models to resolve the problems described in the ERs. Thus in addition to emplotting the micro-narratives, counselors "arch the character." The arc traces an inner journey that describes a client's transformation. Counselors emphasize how coalescing role-model identifications into their own identity during late adolescence and emerging adulthood constitute who they are as well as contribute to who they are becoming.

Assess

The sequential structure of the plot reveals the character arc. Counselor begin discussing the arc by stating the perspective and preoccupations the client revealed in the ERs and then move to discuss how the client chose role models to imitate. For virtually all clients, role model characteristics portray solutions to their early problems and continuing preoccupations. Thus, constructionist counselors must be diligent in understanding and communicating in the life portrait how clients' role models solve the problems articulated in their ERs. For example, consider W.W. the client who recalled feeling alone as she waited for her mother to arrive at the hospital. We learned that her role model of Wonder Woman is always there to help and save people.

> W.W.'s life-portrait sentence 3: *To solve problems in growing up, I turned feeling abandoned into always being available to help those who feel alone in the world.*

Consider another example from an adult woman who worked in the helping professions. *I remember falling into my uncle's pool, not knowing how to swim and falling slowly to the bottom, only to look up and see someone's arm pull me out. I was scared and helpless.* Her first role model was Dorothy from The Wizard of OZ because she was *independent and able to help others achieve what was lacking in their lives. She had the courage to fight the Wicked Witch and travel to an unknown land.* Dorothy modeled independence not helplessness as well as courage not fear. And of course, helping others achieve what is lacking in their lives fits well within the client's occupation.

Some clients make the connection themselves before counselors draw their attention to the link. For example, in describing her heroine Nancy Drew a woman remarked, *I was always impressed with her bravery because I was not a brave kid. She did scary things. I used to marvel that she could go in the dark with a flashlight down the stairs by herself. I am still not as brave as her but I am working on it.*

Tips

Try to show clients a character arc in which they transform the passive suffering in the ERs into active mastery by emulating characteristics of their role models. Strongly reinforce this conceptualization of moving from passive to active and foreshadow how bridging the transition will extend and thicken their character arc.

If you encounter difficulty making connections, write on the left side of a blank sheet of paper the client's first ER and on the right side write role-model attributes. Then draw a line between them to represent the process of turning passive into active. On the line write a statement for the life portrait that explains the line. For example, in an ER a client felt frightened whereas in his role models he admired bravery. The line then states, *You began as a frightened little guy but to survive in this world and accomplish your goals you needed bravery. See how you selected brave heroes You imitated them to turn your fear into courage.*

When possible use parallel words that appear in both the client's ERs and role-model descriptions. For example, with the client who gave the ER headline "Girl Fears Change," I emphasized two phrases from her role model descriptions. One model was described *as able to confront her fears.* A second model was described as *went after what she wanted.* I said to the client, *You fear change yet you have shaped a self that is not afraid to confront your fears and pursue what you want.*

Extend the transformation from passive to active into the transition narrative. Ask clients how their character strengths may now be used to bridge the transition and possibly how they may be used in their next work position.

In the psychology of motivation, there are three prominent constructs: needs, values, and interests (Savickas, 2014). ERs portray needs or what one lacks. Role models reveal values or what one seeks to fulfill their needs. Thus valued goals such as achievement fulfill needs such as overcoming feeling inadequate. The third construct is interests, which connect needs to values.

Task 4. Name Interests

Name the types of occupations or academic majors that fit a client's interests and explain how they implement the attributes that they adopted from their role models

Complete the following life-portrait sentences.

I can now use the attributes that I learned from role models in my educational and vocational pursuits. I am interested in being around people who are _____; places such as _____; solving problems that involve _____; and using procedures like _____. In particular, I am interested in _____, _____, and _____.

Rationale

Constructionist counselors assess the educational and vocational interests that manifest themselves in clients' favorite magazines, television shows, or websites. Descriptions of these vicarious environments suggest clients' preferred work settings and attractive occupations.

Assess

To help clients identify fitting nichés, counselors may analyze along four dimensions the settings that attract client interests. Counselors want to learn the places in which clients want to work, the type of people with whom they wish to interact, the problems that they prefer to address, and the procedures which they like to use. Try assessing the four dimensions for yourself and summarize your own manifest interests. Maybe a sentence such as the following one fits you. "I like being around altruistic and encouraging *people* who work in *places* such as schools and agencies using counseling and advising *procedures* to help people solve career *problems*."

The client W.W. reported enjoying four shows. She liked *Grey's Anatomy because the stories are about people working together to solve problems, overcome adversity, and help other people. There is depth in character development. Each struggles with issues yet has large and small successes.* She liked Community and described it as *a study of a group of misfits.* Also she enjoyed House who is *an outcast in the hospital* and Veronica Mars who is an *outsider in her school.* Her manifest interests suggest the following sentence.

W.W.'s life-portrait sentence 4: *I can now use the attributes I learned from role models in my educational and vocational pursuits. I am interested in being around people who work as a team in*

*places such as schools and hospitals where they
use procedures such as counseling and medicine
to help outcasts solve their problems and overcome adversity. In particular, I may be interested in becoming a psychologist, social worker, or
counselor.*

In assessing manifest interests, counselors may apply Holland's (1997) typology of vocational personalities and work environments. His RIASEC model is a knowledge system that offers a vocabulary of distinctions with which to type people and occupations. The RIASEC vocabulary enables counselors to be more efficient and effective in thinking about individuals and the work world. The six vocational personality and work environment prototypes are incredibly useful in distinguishing the attributes that differentiate work environments and the people who populate them. A brief description of the prototypes follows.

Realistic types are doers who show interest in
   working outdoors or with machines.
Investigative types are thinkers who show
   interest in science and technology.
Artistic types are creators who show interest in
   art, music, and writing.
Social types are helpers who show interest in
   teaching and communicating.
Enterprising types are leaders who show interest
   in managing and persuading.
Conventional types are team members who
   show interest in organizing and maintaining.

Counselors examine and assign types to the descriptions that clients use to account for their attraction to favorite magazines, television programs, and websites. The manifest interests of most clients clearly resemble one or two RIASEC prototypes. For example, W.W. seemed to most resemble the Investigative type who solves problems and the Social type who helps people. The unique attraction for the client may differ from the counselor's general understanding of an object of attention. Nevertheless, for purposes of illustration the following figures show examples of assigning RIASEC types to magazines, television programs, websites, and leisure activities.

Examples of Manifest Interests by RIASEC Type

	Magazines	Television	Websites	Leisure
R	Field and Stream	This Old House	Fine Woodwork	Outdoor Technical Mechanical
I	Science	CSI	NASA	Think Learn Solve
A	Rolling Stone	America's Got Talent	Pandora	Create Write Travel
S	People	Friends	Twitter	Socialize Help Volunteer
E	Money	Shark Tank	Politico	Lead Manage Persuade
C	Coin Collecting	Martha Stewart	Sports Collector Digest	Organize Collect Maintain

Occupational Specialty Interests

Manifest interests may also be used to identify interest in a specialty within an occupation, for instance counseling. Below are examples from six counselors-in-training. Note that each student resembles the Social type yet differs in specialty interests. It is not the title of the magazine or program that reveals interest; it is what the student finds interesting about the magazine or program.

A student planning to become a sex therapist said: *I like* Cosmopolitan *magazine because of the embarrassing discussions of sex.*

A student planning to become a school counselor who works with troubled teenage girls said: *I like* Teen Moms. *It deals with messed up lives and relationships. It is sad and horrible but interesting. I always wish that I could talk with them and help them to see all the toxic things they do and the bad people in their lives.*

A student planning to become a career counselor said: Dr. Who *is always wondering if he is making the right decision and thinks greatly before he does anything.*

A student planning to help individuals make the transition from prison to the community said: *My favorite television show is* Fringe. *It's about parallel worlds. Trying to figure out what is going on in each. The characters want to equal things out and help others figure out for themselves about two worlds.*

A student planning to work with substance abuse clients said: The show The Walking Dead. *It is about people trying to survive. A team that helps each other out.*

A student already working as a career coach said: My husband does not understand why I like The Walking Dead. It is because they remind me of my middle-age clients who have lost their jobs.

Tips

Consult the O*Net to compose a list of occupations that match the client's two-letter or three-letter RIASEC type (https://www.onetonline.org/explore/interests/). Discuss the list with the client and then give it to the client to keep.

Indicate continuity and coherence in interests by tracing how a client's previous academic majors, occupational positions, and leisure pursuits express the interests discussed during this consultation.

Task 5. Script a Scenario

Translate a client's current favorite story in terms of the transition problem and suggest how it may outline a possible course or action for the next scenario in the career story.

Complete the fifth life-portrait topic sentence, namely the scenario sentence: *If I adopt the script from my favorite story, then I will _____ .*

Rationale

Stories can serve as a lens through which people perceive and understand events that they experience. A favorite story reflects back to them aspects of the discourse in which they themselves are embedded. By inserting themselves and their circumstances into that story, they can transform their sense of self; especially when the story suggests a reasonable way in which they may proceed.

Assess

A favorite story comforts clients as they learn how another person resolved a similar problem and how they themselves might move forward. Counselors listen to discern whether a clients' narration of their favorite story suggests a plan for bridging the transition. Counselors are often surprised at how clearly the favorite story suggests a scenario for the next chapter in the career. However, this is no coincidence. The story is a favorite because the client implicitly knows it offers direction that may guide the way they will live in the next chapter of their life story.

W.W. said her favorite movie is <u>Running with Scissors</u>. She described it *as a true story about a dysfunctional family similar to yet worse than mine. The kids had to fend for themselves. The mother had mental issues, was neglectful and abusive. The father left. I want to help children who have been neglected or abandoned as I felt as a child.*

> W.W.'s scenario sentence 5: *If I adopt the script from my favorite story, then I will help children who have been neglected or abandoned by dysfunctional families.*

Example one. A young man who graduated from an Ivy League school three years earlier had been building a successful career in marketing. Nevertheless, he longed for an adventure out West. He also wanted to help others. Notice how his favorite story is changing to fit his new direction.

I have been floundering for a new one lately. I have watched this movie over and over again and read this book over and over again. And I recently watched it and it kind of turned me off and I don't know why. It is <u>Into the Wild</u>. This dude graduates from a prestigious college and gets a job. He saves $20,000. His family wants to buy him a car, and he says *"no I don't want any of that."* He donates all his money to charity and hitchhikes across the country and then goes up to Alaska. He ate too much of a bad plant and it poisoned him and he starved to death up there. Last thing in this movie is he writes this quote. *"Happiness is shared."* I do believe in that quote. When I watched the last time, I thought he was a selfish and angry kid. Why did you have to go through all that and hurt your parents, and hurt your family, and hurt your friends so much to come to that conclusion. I don't think that was necessary. It is selfish to go off and have all these experiences and not share or give back to your community. Giving back is important.

His scenario sentence read, *If I adopt the script from my favorite story, then I will go on an adventure that does not hurt my family and helps others in some community.*

He secured a new job working with a company that provided wilderness expeditions as a therapeutic intervention. He planned to someday open his own therapeutic wilderness program.

Example two. A 28-year old assistant manager at a large company wanted to return to school to learn a new profession but her parents told her to keep her secure job. Her female boss told her that she should stay with the company because she was in line for two promotions with big pay raises. She questioned whether she should leave or not. When asked about her favorite story, she replied,

A Disney movie called Tangled. *A twist on* Rapunzel. *The main character is locked-up in a tower. The mom that she has claims to be her mom but is actually a witch who is trying to contain her because her hair has magical powers. And all she wants to do is venture out into the real world to see what it is like because she has never been able to live outside of those castle walls. She goes on this whole* journey of self-discovery and then discovers that this person who she thought was her mom is actually this evil witch. She is a part of a royal family and has been missing for years and years. In the end, she is reunited with her family. It is liberating when her magical hair is cut off. At first she thought it was terrible, then she realized that it was what kept her in danger her whole life because that was what people were after her whole life.

Her scenario sentence read, *If I adopt the script from my favorite story, then I will leave the castle and test my magic powers for healing others.*

While discussing her favorite story, it dawned on her that her female boss acted as a witch that was trying to keep her at the company. With this insight, she burst into laughter. She then wondered when she left the company if she would lose her "magical powers." She worked up the courage to quit the company and enrolled in nursing school where her magic powers could heal people.

Example three. A male counseling student wondered whether he should pursue a doctorate. He worked full-time and took two master's degree courses at night. At work, he had difficulty saying no to requests, causing him to work 10-15 hours per week more than required. His fiancée complained that she never saw him.

My favorite books are <u>Lord of the Rings</u>. *My favorite part is the precursor. It is about the creation of the world in the middle earth. It centers around a character who is gifted and he creates something that is stolen by the devil figure and the rest of the book is his ambition to retrieve the stolen object. In the process of pursuing his obsession, he loses his friends and family.*

His scenario sentence read, *If I adopt the script from my favorite story, then I will balance my career ambition with time for family and friends.*

Fearing that his ambition would cost him his engagement and marriage, he secured a graduate assistantship, quit his demanding job, and practiced saying no assertively.

Example four. A 45 year old man wanted to discuss his dream job and whether he should move to it. He had a secure job that he liked yet did not love

Das Boots *is my favorite book and movie. It's about a World War II submarine. It's an against all odds sort of thing. Being at sea. I identified with the chief engineer. At one point in the movie they have been hit by a big shell. They are stuck in the bottom of the ocean. Have to get water out of boat. Limited oxygen so they cannot stay down long. They know they are going to die. Chief engineer says everything is ready. They have one chance to blow to the surface. Everybody has energy again. There is all this tension, but it works and everyone survives.*

His scenario sentence read, *If I adopt the script from my favorite story, then I will take what feels like my last chance to surface my true passion in a new occupation.*

In discussing the story he said, *My current career is pacifying some jerks. It's deadening. It's just so true! I am stuck at the bottom. I have one last chance to pursue my dream. If I stay where I am, I will continue to suffocate until I retire. I want the challenge.*

Tips

Position the story in relation to a client's response to the entry question, *How can I be useful to you?* The story probably implicitly answers the question that brought the client to counseling.

Consider how the script may contain characters or objects

that serve as metaphors. For example, a client's favorite story was *Pride and Prejudice*. She described the possible marriage to Mr. Collins as offering security and stability, whereas the possible marriage to Mr. Darcy offers excitement, mystery, and non-conformity. The counselor said, *Your current career path leads to an occupation named Collins yet you yearn for an occupation named Darcy.*

Career construction counselors define identity as self in a social role. Try to portray the client as using the script to perform self in a new occupational role, thereby revising vocational identity.

Not all clients change occupation, job, or academic major. It is possible that they can remain in their current position or organization because counseling has reaffirmed a world of meaning that had been challenged in some way. These clients, now better able to perceive meaning and preserve their self-esteem, change the role played in their position or organization.

Task 6. Apply Advice

Pinpoint how the advice proffered in a client's favorite saying could direct and propel the client's initial action to bridge the transition.

Complete the sixth life-portrait topic sentence: *The best advice I have for myself right now is _____.*

Rationale

Favorite sayings condense experience into practical wisdom. They offer useful guidance regarding clients' circumstances, and usually suggest tactical action that could begin to bridge the transition.

The process of considering their advice to themselves reinforces clients' authority in authoring their own lives. It builds confidence because they realize that the answers to their questions are within them, not provided by the counselor as expert.

Assess

Clients' advice to themselves usually makes immediate sense; rarely does it not fit the life portrait being sketched. It is something very important that the client knows, yet does not apprehend. Sometimes it is referred to as the "unthought known."

Consider the advice as coming from the play's director who guides the client to perform life in the wake of the transition, both in the backstage of private meaning and on the front stage of public enactment (Neimeyer, 2012). As in the theater, the director interprets the script and communicates to the client the action required to play the role. W.W. advised herself, *It is not about waiting for the storm to pass, it is about learning to dance in the rain.* When asked what this saying meant to her, she replied that she must stop dwelling in the past and get on with her own life so she is better able to help others.

> W.W.'s life portrait sentence 6: *The best advice I have for myself right now is stop waiting for the storm to pass and start learning to dance in the rain.*

Note that in her ER, her first verb was *waiting*. Her advice to herself is to stop waiting.

Examples from clients:

- If it's going to be, it's up to me.
- When a door closes a window opens.
- God hates a coward.
- You are not a loser until you stop trying.
- Choose courage not comfort.

Task 7. Unify the Life Portrait

Assemble and edit the life-portrait sentences into a verbal portrait that depicts the client's career with continuity and coherence.

In facing this transition, my underlying concern is _____. *It reminds me of my feelings of* _____. *To solve my problems in growing up I became* _____, _____, *and* _____. *These attributes are important in my next position. They formed my character by turning* _____ *into* _____. *Given the self that I have built, I like being around similar people who are* _____ *and* _____. *I like places such as* _____ *and* _____. *I prefer using procedures like* _____ *in solving problems such as* _____. *If I adopt the script from my favorite story, then I will* _____. *The best advice I have for myself right now is* _____.

Rationale

Counselors produce a first draft of the life portrait by consolidating the sentences that they have written in Tasks 1 through 6. The composite portrays the reconstructed story, provides a superordinate view of the transition, and envisions future possibilities.

Assess

After composing a life portrait, counselors must assess how well the depiction addresses the client's reason for seeking consultation. The portrait must be comprehensible and credible in responding to the problems in the transition narrative and in articulating what the client is calling for in the next career scenario.

In reviewing the first draft of the life portrait, counselors ensure that it clearly describes the client in three ways (Savickas, 2002).

- a social actor who plays a character (role model question)
- a motivated agent who pursues goals in a context (magazine/television show/website question)
- an autobiographical author who scripts a performance (favorite story question)

Then counselors edit the portrait to emphasize animating themes and the client's character arc. These elements are important in helping clients to appreciate their progressive realization of wholeness and form intentions for the future.

Tips

The life-portrait sentences produced by the six tasks may each be used as a topic sentence for a paragraph that elaborates an idea. The paragraph may describe the topic in more detail, offer further explanation, or provide substantiating facts and examples.

Give the best possible account, infusing the portrait with values and dignity.

Let the client's life speak for itself.

Highlight the metaphors used by the client to open new perspectives.

In editing the portrait, make it internally consistent and use the same or similar language throughout.

Add transitions where appropriate to connect the parts and have the sentences flow seamlessly.

Chapter Five

Counseling Process

During the first session, constructionist counselors conduct the Career Construction Interview. During the second session, they present clients with a draft of their reconstructed career story and engage in narrative counseling to co-construct plans. Counselors may begin the second session by chatting with clients. Following a brief warm-up, counselors ask clients, *Has anything become clearer to you since we last met?* If clients offer something important, then counselors remember to insert it into the life portrait. Next counselors restate how clients had said counseling might be useful to them. At this point, counselors begin to narrate the life portrait in a clear and crisp manner.

Part One: Retelling the Story

Goal

Have clients hear their life portraits and reflect upon what they know implicitly yet have not made explicit to themselves or announced to other people.

Rationale

Counselors retell clients' stories emplotted in a life portrait, while also enriching the story with their own commentary. A good retelling prompts clients to purposefully re-engage with their identities and relationships. As counselors retell the macro-narrative following the life-portrait's sequential plot (perspective, self-concept, interests, script, advice), they guide the process toward the boundary (Buhler, 1935) of clients' experience and understanding. They enhance clients' sense of agency by helping them to appreciate the coherence and continuity in their stories. Counselors always emphasize the most adaptive behaviors that the client is capable of achieving.

Counselors proceed slowly and pause after each segment. They encourage clients to hold the portrait in mind as they reflect and self-explore. Counselors want clients to dwell in their stories and begin to envision possibilities. They unlock meaning not impose it.

Counselors look for evidence that clients recognize themselves in their portraits and take possession of who they are. Verbal expressions of agreement are fine yet abstract. Counselors look for acknowledgement of the life portrait's usefulness in concrete bodily expressions of felt recognition including involuntary, spontaneous reactions such as smiles, tears, blushing, and laughter

Process

Throughout the retelling, counselors use silence to provide space for deliberation and empathic responding to focus attention. They continuously prompt clients to engage in retrospective reflection about past experiences and prospective reflexivity about the future. Reflection involves a more passive recollection that clients use to learn about themselves whereas reflexivity involves a more active conceptualization that clients use to change themselves in some way (Savickas, 2016).

Counselors begin a retelling with the perspective from the first ER to set the scene and create a context for the dialogue. They read the first headline and summarize the vignette to help clients begin to think about the story in a different way. Counselors are keenly aware that the ERs are memories about the present for the future. ERs describe issues that clients need to deal with during CCC.

Together client and counselor deconstruct any haunting assumptions or self-negating beliefs. If the ER contains constricting and dominating accounts, counselors help to disrupt them and develop new understandings. Deconstructing difficult meanings in ERs involves a sense-breaking that moves the client to view experiences differently, question underlying assumptions, and reconsider their meaning. After fully attending to the first ER, counselors in turn discuss and deconstruct the remaining two ERs. As a part of deconstructing a self-negating idea, counselors increase clients' sense of agency by externalizing the issue (White & Epson, 1990). They convince clients that they are not the problem, the problem is the problem.

After discussing each ER in turn, counselors then unify them, if possible, by reading the three headlines one after another showing how the headlines actually tell a story in and of themselves. Often the sequence of headlines can be read (from first to third or from third to first) as movement from passive to active along a three-part sequence of issue, intensification, and resolution. This step in the retelling typically sets a perspective and introduces a theme that will be traced in going forward.

Having identified the perspective and a thematic issue, counselors turn to discussing the attributes depicted by the client's role models. This retelling helps clients understand why a hero or heroine was so important to them, and how they have incorporated into their self-construction the very attributes that they most admired. This goes beyond reminding clients of their self-concept and competencies. The aim is to describe how the client needed these characteristics to solve problems in growing up; and, thus why the client incorporated them in their self-construction. The attributes are explicitly linked to the ERs. For example, if an ER ripples with fear, then the role models respond with courage. If an ER depicts loneliness, then the role models display sociability. If an ER implicates chaos, then the role models impose order. This pattern of reversal is the essence of the character arc. In short, counselors help clients understand how they have constructed a self who they themselves needed. They have become the person who they wish had been there to help them when they were children. Counselors highlight the ways in which the client has transformed passivity into activity. What was empty is now being filled.

Following discussion of self-construction, counselors turn clients' attention to their vocational interests. They describe a client's unique attraction to a work content and position as an attempt to place the character on a fitting stage to perform the self. Constructionist counselors view vocational identity as a performance (LaPointe, 2010). Remember that identity means self in a role.

After describing the client's unique interests and aspirations, counselors find that many clients have identified the occupation that they wish to pursue. For clients who still seem uncertain, counselors compose and discuss a list of congruent occupations based on their appraisal of clients' manifest interests and RIASEC codes. Counselors explain to clients that they resemble in many ways people who work in the listed occupations. Because people make the place and form the occupation, clients may wish to explore how well they fit the requirements, routines, and rewards of the listed occupations.

Having staged their character by placing the self in a setting, it is time to outline a scenario that clients may be preparing to enact on that occupational stage. The current favorite story from a movie or book is now retold with the client as the central character. Counselors read back the client's exact words in describing the favorite story, and watch for client bodily expressions of felt recognition. The script usually contains the answer to the questions that clients brought to counseling. Clients had expected that the counselor would answer those questions, and now are surprised as well as pleased to learn that they themselves had the answers all along.

Counselors should vividly explain to clients that their favorite saying instructs them in how to begin performing the new scene. Counselors may continue to use the script metaphor and explain the advice as the director guiding the actor. Of course in this instance actors direct themselves.

At this point in the process, counselors may summarize what has been accomplished so far. Together, client and counselor have answered the following questions about the client.

Who are you? (role models)
Where do you want to work? (magazines/tv/web)
What do you want to do there? (scenario)
Why you want to do it? (ERs)
How should you begin? (saying)

Tips

Read the life portrait in a manner that turns passive suffering into active mastery.

Point to parallels between self-concept and vocational identity.

Watch for and explore emotions, sighs, silences, and insights.

Part Two: Action Planning

Now it is time to return to clients' response to the entry question of how counselling might be useful to them. Together client and counselor consider whether discussing the life portrait accomplished what the client initially sought from counseling.

In an effort to stabilize the new narrative so the changed story takes hold and becomes permanent, counselors prompt clients to discern the difference between the old story and the anticipated story as well as conceptualize the process by which they themselves have authored and authorized the change. In conceptualizing the process of change, clients can realize they are both the actor in and author of the change process. At this point, clients often feel an emotional grounding that enables them to anticipate enacting their plan and personal agency to mobilize action.

Intentionality

Next, counselors move clients to articulate their new intentions. The tension that clients felt at the beginning of counseling has resolved through the attention paid to it. Clients no longer feel lost and confused because they have viewed their transition from a new perspective, gained cognitive insights, and increased emotional awareness. These developments have moved them to more explicitly realize their intentions, thereby enhancing their ability to make commitments even in circumstances of uncertainty.

Fostering intentionality is a goal of CCC, so counselors pause to recognize this accomplishment. As part of reinforcing a client's intentionality, counselors communicate to clients that their intentions are important both in the present circumstance as well as in the future when they will again cross a transition in the world of temporary jobs.

Planning

Having clarified purpose and declared intentions, clients then set goals that chart a direction through possibilities and constraints. Client and counselor co-construct a plan for strategic changes and tactical actions that can test the provisional understandings generated during counseling. A client's plan to bridge the transition usually is quite obvious after discussing the life portrait. What had been implicit has been made explicit. Clients themselves know what needs to be done, and counseling has substantiated it. Most often, a plan involves the client moving beyond prior boundaries, set either by self or other people. Typical plans may include one or more of the following deliberate actions: confirming intentions, exploring choices, asserting self with parents or partners, applying to an academic program or for an occupational position, resigning a positon, moving to a new city, or entering clinical counseling about an issue that needs working through over time. To inspire hope, all plans should include alternatives in case they are needed.

Audience

Almost every action plan should include clients telling their re-authored stories to important audiences. Because clients will play new roles in concert with others, they must learn how well the company of close relationships will accommodate the revised story. Clients should attempt to secure the validation of relevant audiences and marshal social resources toward the performance of new roles. Thus, counselors encourage clients to ground their new stories in a secure base by narrating it to an audience of family, mentors, and close friends. Hopefully, these audiences -- especially the necessary other -- will support the new story, encourage its performance, and even forge a more-or-less revised relationship with the client. To learn more about the role of audience in CCC consult Briddick and Sensoy-Briddick (2013).

Narratability

Narratability is not the narrative; it is a client's ability to recite the new story to audiences. Increasing clients' narratability is another goal of CCC. Being able to articulate a life purpose is strongly associated with life satisfaction (Bronk, Hill, Lapsley, Talib, Finch, 2009). To strengthen clients' ability to narrate their re-authored stories counselors may have clients rehearse. Telling one's story should not be self-centered. It involves knowing the audience and performing a telling that they can recognize. There will be audience reactions and maybe even surprises. As in the theater, a receptive audience energizes performance of the narrative. If client and counselor anticipate hesitant or negative reactions from an audience member, then they prepare responses.

Action

But more than a plan and rehearsal are needed; actions must be taken. Clients need to audition their new roles. They must inhabit their stories and perform them in order to answer the questions that brought them to counseling. The meaning of a new story comes into being when it is enacted in the real world. Re-authored identity stories become transformative in their performance. Only through action will clients truly answer for themselves questions such as, *What suits me now? What do I want to do? What can I do?*

Tips

Encouragement. With a tentative plan formulated, counselors turn their attention to reinforcing optimism and mobilizing action. Although clients may know what they need to do, it often takes courage at the crossroads. Accordingly, clients muster efforts toward successful performance on the stage of the social world. Counselors incite effort by shifting from empathic responding to encouragement. Empathy denotes counselor responses from the perspective of the client. In empathic responding the counselor may say, *You feel* _____ *because you* _____. Encouragement denotes responses from the perspective of the counselor. An encouraging statement might be, *I believe that you can do it.* Encouragement becomes increasingly important after the retelling of the life portrait. My favorite book on learning to respond with encouragement is *Encouraging Children to Learn* by Dreikurs and Dinkmeyer (2000).

Information Seeking. If the plan involves advanced exploration, counselors may teach clients the general information-seeking behaviors: observe, visit, listen, talk, write, read, and google. Some counselors use a handout with these words printed down a left column. Together client and counselor brainstorm to list specific actions that the client may be willing to take in as many of the seven categories as reasonable. Clients are asked to keep notes on what they learn from the exploration and what it means to them in terms of advantages and disadvantages.

Realism. Counselors encourage clients to take agentic action in pursuit of a life that they want to live. Counselors enhance client agency using language and perspectives that change the meaning of things and offer a sense of possibility and progress. However, there are limits that define and confine clients' capacity to choose freely. Each person pushes against the unchosen conditions of their life. There are normative boundaries and social constraints that both precede and exceed the client. Usually the best a client can do is to improvise and compose a life with the available resources and social supports. Certainly, they can make commitments to self and then choose the best possible solutions for self and others. Sometimes, or maybe all the time, choices are about progress not perfection. With a commitment to social justice, counselors encourage client volition to push against normative boundaries and social constraints to achieve for themselves, and maybe others, the best possible choice and most vital life design.

Closing Session Two

To complete the second session, counselors read aloud the client's response to the entry question of how counseling could be useful and then ask the client, *Have we done that?* When the answer is yes, the session is complete and the counselor sets an appointment for the client to return in a month to report the results of plan enactment.

W.W. originally answered the entry question of how counseling could be useful as follows.

> *I am ready to return to work but I need a little bit of direction right now. I get very worried and anxious about not having a path and knowing where I am going. I do not quite fit into the mode of a 4th grade teacher anymore. In my senior year in high school I wanted to go into psychology. I just connected with everything my high school psychology teacher said. I kind of got attached. I really connected to what she said. I loved talking about relationships. I went away to college and majored in psychology. But during my first year I had panic attacks because I was alone. I had a big group of friends at home but none at college. I knew I made a mistake so I came home. Because I failed my first year in college, I shifted my major from psychology to education. I graduated and went to work as a teacher until I had my son. He is now going to enter the first grade and I want to return to work. I just wonder if there is something better for me than teaching. I want to do more than that. I am struggling to find something that I would be happy doing the rest of my life. I am confused. I am thinking of going to graduate*

school to study school counseling, but I wonder can I handle graduate school. Will I be able to do what is required of me? So that is what I came to you for. Sometimes I think that school counseling is the right avenue for me but maybe I should just return to teaching.

A life portrait that combines her answers to the scaffolding questions follows.

In facing this transition, my underlying concern has reminded me that I fear being alone and abandoned. I do not want to make a wrong choice and be trapped waiting for something better. It reminds me of feeling isolated and upset. To solve problems in growing up, I turned feeling abandoned into always being available to help those who feel alone in the world. I am strong, caring, and helpful. I always protect the innocent but not in a violent way. These attributes are important in my next position. I can now use the attributes I learned from role models in my educational and vocational pursuits. I am interested in being around people who work as a team in places such as schools and hospitals where they use procedures such as counseling and medicine to help outcasts solve their problems and overcome adversity. I want to give a Sprite to misfits and outsiders. If I adopt the plot from my favorite story, then I will help children who have been neglected or abandoned by dysfunctional families. In particular, I may enjoy working as a psychologist, social worker, or counselor. The best advice I have for myself right now is to stop waiting for the storm to pass and start learning to dance in the rain so I can help children do the same.

It became obvious that she wanted to attend graduate school to study psychology, not school counseling.

I want to help lost people. I want to work with people who don't have many friends or family. However, I do not want to work with homeless people or battered women because I am too emotional. I am physically and mentally strong though. I want to work as a part of a team.

When I asked what stops her from just deciding to go to graduate school, she said:

I want to be a good mother. I fear abandonment. I am afraid that if I do not play with my son that he will feel abandoned.

The issue had first appeared in her transition narrative. She had said that she wondered whether she would be able to do what graduate school would require of her. The client was not daunted by the intellectual work of academia, but haunted by a fear of being away from her son too long. She has now explained to the counselor and herself what is at stake in choosing a career path. As a single mother, she does not want to abandon her son. And just as importantly, she does not want him to abandon her because she spends too much time in activities required by graduate school.

With cresting emotions, she discussed her options frankly. She dreamed of a doctorate in clinical psychology yet believed that it would take too much time away from her son. After some discussion and information gathering, she quickly and confidently decided to pursue a M.A. in school psychology, which she perceived as both less demanding and quicker than a doctorate in clinical psychology. Moreover, it would build on her teaching experience. Furthermore, it would leave the door open for her to later pursue a doctorate in school psychology. We discussed how she would narrate her new story to her young son and recruit the help of her ex-husband, parents, and friends.

During graduate school she was able to balance assignments with quality time for her son. After graduating she secured a position as a school psychologist in a pediatric hospital where she worked with school systems to help long-term patients do their assignments and keep connected with their peers. Eventually, she shifted her duties to become a child psychologist and family therapist in the hospital's psychiatry department. In the end, she successfully mastered what she had passively suffered by helping children in the way she herself once needed.

Goodbye

Constructionist counselors say goodbye by repeating clients' favorite sayings to them as they prepare to leave. They rarely close with a compliment or appreciation for the work performed. Rather, they propel forward movement and honor the client's own wisdom by repeating the favorite saying. To W.W. I said, *It's time to stop waiting to go to graduate school to learn how to help children dance in the rain.*

After clients leave the consulting room they must make something happen. We know the world by taking action and seeing what happens. Agentic action consists of behaviors that individuals perform as a way of constructing meaning for themselves. In addition to making meaning, agentic action often creates opportunities and validates self-authorization.

Session Three

Many clients do not need a third session. They inform their counselors by e-mail or telephone that things have worked-out well. The clients who do keep the appointment usually report their findings, receive reassurance, and discuss a next step or two. Occasionally, a client will report that the actions taken closed a door they hoped to enter. Then the alternatives come into play. Client and counselor discuss them and craft a new action plan. This does not occur very often yet counselors should not be surprised when it does because the world does not always cooperate with clients.

Evaluating Process and Outcome

To increase their knowledge and improve their practice, counselors evaluate both the process and outcomes of their counseling. To evaluate CCC outcomes the central question addressed involves the effectiveness of the intervention in achieving client goals (Gibson & Cartwright, 2014). I do this after the second session by administering the *Session Rating Scale* (Shaw & Murray, 2014) to assess client goal-attainment and satisfaction. To evaluate narrative outcomes, I use the *Future Career Autobiography* (Rehfuss, 2009). To measure client reflection as an outcome of counseling, I use the Self-Exploration Scale from the *Career Exploration Survey* (Stumpf, Colarelli, & Hartmann, 1983). To evaluate process, I use the *Innovative Moments Coding System* (Cardoso, Silva, Gocalves, & Duarte, 2014a & 2014b). Together these methods for evaluating process and outcome provide important feedback for my continuing professional development.

Postscript

The CCC model offers counselors a set of narrative methods to enhance their practice. Expertise in the use of these techniques and knowledge about career construction develops with experience. Counselors improve their skill in using the techniques with each session, and there is no endpoint. After decades of doing CCC, I still learn something new from each and every client, and so will you. After all, clients are our best teachers.

If you would like to learn more about CCC, you may practice with clients by using two free resources available at www.Vocopher.com: *My Career Story* (Savickas & Hartung, 2012) and the *Career Construction Interview Form* (Savickas, 2013). For advanced study of career constructing as a narrative intervention, practitioners may consult an article that explains innovative moments in the construction of career change (Cardosa, Savickas, & Gonçalves, 2019).

The American Psychological Association has published a book on counseling for career construction (Savickas, 2019) and two DVDs that show live demonstrations of the intervention. The first DVD shows CCC completed in a single session (Savickas, 2006). The second DVD (Savickas, 2009) shows three sessions each for the cases of Ryan and Michael, which were analyzed separately by Cardoso, Silva, Gonçalves, and Duarte (2014a, 2014b) using the Innovative Moments Model. The case of Ryan was also analyzed by Taveira, Ribeiro, Cardoso, and Silva (2017) using the Therapeutic Collaboration Coding System to demontrate how collaboratin becomes therapeutic.

Additional reading may include the following books and articles.

Busacca, L. A., & Rehfuss, M. C. (Eds.) (2016). *Postmodern career counselling: A handbook of culture, context, and cases.* Hoboken, NJ: Wiley.

DiFabio, A. & Maree, J. G. (2013). *Psychology of career counseling: New challenges for a new era.* New York: Nova Science Publishers.

Hartung, P. J. (2013). Career as story: Making the narrative turn. In W. B. Walsh & M. L. Savickas, & P. J. Hartung (Eds.) *Handbook of vocational psychology* (4th ed.). Mahwah, NJ: Lawrence Erlbaum Associates.

Hartung, P. J., & Santilli, S. (2017). My Career Story: Description and initial validity evidence. *Journal of Career Assessment, 26,* 1-14.

Hartung, P., & Vess, L. (2019). Career construction for life design: Practice and theory. In N. Arthur & M. McMahon (Eds.). *Contemporary theories of career development: International perspectives* (pp. 91-104). New York: Routledge.

Nota, L., & Rossier, J. (Eds.) (2015). *Handbook of life design.* Gottingen, Germany: Hogrefe

Obi, O. P. (2015). Constructionist career counseling of undergraduate students: An experimental evaluation. *Journal of Vocational Behavior, 88,* 215-219.

Savickas, M. L. (2015). Career counseling paradigms: Guiding, developing, and designing. In P. Hartung, M. Savickas, W. Walsh (Eds.) *APA handbook of career intervention* (Vol. 1: Foundations, pp. 129-143). Washington, DC: APA Books.

Savickas, M. L. (2020). Career construction theory and practice. In R. W. Lent & S. D. Brown (Eds.). *Career development and counseling: Putting theory and research to work* (3rd ed.). Hoboken, New Jersey: John Wiley.

Savickas, M. L., & Guichard, J. (Eds.) (2016). Special issue: Reflexivity in life designing interventions. *Journal of Vocational Behavior, 97,* 1-88.

References

Angus, L. E. Greenberg, L. S. (2011). *Working with narrative in emotion-focused therapy: Changing stories, healing lives*. Washington, DC: American Psychological Association.

Arnold, M. B. (1962). *Story sequence analysis: A new method of measuring motivation and predicting achievement*. New York: Columbia University Press.

Bollas, C. (1987). *The shadow of the object: Psychoanalysis of the unthought known*. New York: Columbia University Press.

Bordin, E. S. (1979). The generalizability of the psychoanalytic concept of the working alliance. *Psychotherapy: Theory, Research & Practice, 16*, 252-260.

Briddick, W. C. & Sensoy-Briddick, H. (2013). The role of audience in life design. In A. DiFabio & J. G. Maree (Eds.). *Psychology of career counselling: New challenges for a new era* (pp. 69-81). New York: Nova.

Bronk, K. C., Hill, P. L., Lapsley, D. K., Talib, T. L., Finch, H. (2009). Purpose, hope, and life satisfaction in three age groups. *Journal of Positive Psychology, 4*, 500-510.

Buhler, C. (1935). *From birth to maturity: An outline of the psychological development of the child*. London: Kegan Paul, Trench, Tubner.

Cardoso, P., Savickas, M. L., & Goncalves, M. M. (2019). Innovative moments in career construction counseling: Proposal for an integrative model. *Career Development Quarterly*, 188-204.

Cardoso, P., Silva, J. R., Gocalves, M. M., & Duarte, M. E. (2014a). Innovative moments and change in Career Construction Counseling. *Journal of Vocational Behavior, 84*,

11-20.

Cardoso, P., Silva, J. R., Gocalves, M.M., & Duarte, M. E. (2014b). Narrative innovation in life design counseling: The case of Ryan. *Journal of Vocational Behavior, 85,* 276–286.

Carkhuff, R. R. (1969). *Helping and human relations: A primer for lay and professional helpers.* New York: Holt, Rinehart and Winston.

Clark, A. (2002). *Early recollections: Theory and practice in counseling and psychotherapy.* New York: Routledge.

Davies, B. & Harre, R. (1990). Positioning: Conversation and the production of selves. *Journal for the Theory of Social Behavior, 20,* 43-63.

Dreikurs, R., & Dinkmeyer, D. (2000). *Encouraging children to learn.* New York: Routledge.

Erikson, E. (1968). *Identity: Youth and crisis.* New York: Norton.

Forster, E. M. (1985). *Aspects of the novel.* New York: Mariner Books (original work published 1927).

Gibson, K., & Cartwright, C. (2014). Young clients' narratives of the purpose and outcome of counselling. *British Journal of Guidance and Counselling, 42,* 511-524.

Holland, J. L. (1997). *Making vocational choices: A theory of vocational personalities and work environments.* Lutz, FL: Psychological Assessment Resources.

Kashdam, T. B., Barrett, l. F., & McKnight, P. E. (2015). Unpacking emotion differentiation: Transforming unpleasant experience by perceiving distinctions in negativity. *Current Directions in Psychological Science, 24,* 10-16.

Kelly, G. A. (1955). *The psychology of personal constructs.* New York: Norton.

Kolb, D. A. (1984). *Experiential learning: Experience as the source of learning and development* (Vol. 1). Englewood Cliffs, NJ: Prentice-Hall.

LaPointe, K. (2010). Narrating career, positioning identity: Career identity as a narrative practice. *Journal of Vocational Behavior, 77,* 1-9.

Leitner, L.M., & Faidley, A. J. (2003, August). *Emotion and the creation of meaning: An experiential constructivist approach.* Paper presented at the American Psychological Association Convention. Toronto, Canada.

Leising, D., Scharloth, J., Lohse, O., & Wood, D. (2014) What types of terms do people use when describing an individual's personality? *Psychological Science 25,* 1787-1794.

Madigan, S. (2011). *Narrative therapy.* Washington, DC: American Psychological Association.

Madill, A., Sermpezis, C., & Barkham, M. (2005). Interactional positioning and narrative self-construction in the first session of psychodynamic-interpersonal psychotherapy. *Psychotherapy Research, 15,* 420-432.

Matlis, S., & Christianson, M. (2014). Sense-making in organizations: Taking stock and moving forward. *Academy of Management Annals, 8,* 57-125.

Mayman, M., & Faris, M. (1960). Early memories as an expression of relationship patterns. *American Journal of Orthopsychiatry, 30,* 507-520.

Mosak, H. H. (1958) Early recollections as a projective technique. *Journal of Projective Techniques, 22,* 302-311.

Neimeyer, R. A. (2012). From stage follower to stage manager: Contemporary directions in bereavement care. In K. J. Doka & A. S. Tucci (Eds.), *Beyond Kübler Ross: New perspectives on death, dying and grief* (pp. 129-150).

Washington, DC: Hospice Foundation of America.

Rehfuss, M. (2009). The Future Career Autobiography: A narrative measure of career intervention effectiveness. *Career Development Quarterly, 58,* 82-90.

Rennie, D. L. (2012). Qualitative research as methodological hermeneutics. *Psychological Methods, 17,* 385-398.

Savickas, M. L. (2002). Career construction: A developmental theory of vocational behavior. In D. Brown (Ed.), *Career choice and development* (4th ed., pp. 149-205). San Francisco: Jossey-Bass.

Savickas, M. L. (2006). Career counseling. (Treatments for Specific Populations Video Series). Washington, DC: American Psychological Association.

Savickas, M. L. (2009). Career counseling over time. (Psychotherapy in Six Sessions Video Series). Washington, DC: American Psychological Association.

Savickas, M. L. (2011). *Career counseling.* Washington, DC: American Psychological Association.

Savickas, M. L. (2012). Life design: A paradigm for career intervention in the 21st century. *Journal of Counseling and Development, 90,* 13-19.

Savickas, M. L. (2013). *Career Construction Interview.* www.Vocopher.com

Savickas, M. L. (2014). Work values: A career construction elaboration. In M. Pope, L. Flores, & P. Rottinghaus (Eds.). *Values in vocational psychology* (pp. 3-19). Charlotte, NC: Information Age Publishing.

Savickas, M. L. (2015a). Career counseling paradigms: Guiding, developing, and designing. In P. Hartung, M. Savickas, & W. Walsh (Eds.) *The APA handbook of career intervention* (Vol. 1, pp. 129-143). Washington, DC: APA Books.

Savickas, M. L. (2015b). Designing projects for career construction. In R. A. Young, J. F. Domene, & L. Valach (Eds.), *Counseling and action: Toward life-enhancing work, relationships, and identity* (pp. 13-31). New York: Springer Science+Business Media.

Savickas, M. L. (2016). Reflection and reflexivity during life-design intervention: Comments on Career Construction Counseling. *Journal of Vocational Behavior, 97*, 84-89.

Savickas, M. L. (2019). *Career counseling* (2nd ed.). Washington, DC: American Psychological Association Press.

Savickas, M. L. (2020). Career construction theory and practice. In R. W. Lent & S. D. Brown (Eds.). *Career development and counseling: Putting theory and research to work* (3rd ed.). Hoboken, New Jersey: John Wiley & Sons.

Savickas, M. L., & Hartung. P. J. (2012). *My Career Story.* www.Vocopher.com

Savickas, M. L., Nota, L., Rossier, J., Dauwalder, J. P., Duarte, M. E., Guichard, J., Soresi, S., Van Esbroeck, R. & van Vianen, A. E. M. (2009). Life designing: A paradigm for career construction in the 21st century. *Journal of Vocational Behavior, 75*, 239-250.

Shaw, S., L., & Murrary, K. W. (2014). Monitoring alliance and outcome with client feedback measures. *Journal of Mental Health Counseling, 36*, 43-57.

Stern, D. N. (2004). *The present moment in sychotherapy and everyday life.* New York: Norton.

Stiles, W. B., Leiman, M., Shapiro, D. A., Hardy, G. E., Barkham, M., Detert, N. B., & Llewelyn, S. P. (2006). What does the first exchange tell? Dialogical sequence analysis and assimilation in very brief therapy. *Psychotherapy Research, 16*, 408-421.

Stumpf, S. A., Colarelli, S. M., & Hartmann, K. (1983). Development of the Career Exploration Survey (CES). *Journal of Vocational Behavior, 22*, 191-226.

Taveira, M. C., Ribeiro, E., Cardoso, P. & Silva, F. (2017). The therapeutic collaboration in life design counselling: The case of Ryan. *South African Journal of Education, 37*, 1-12.

Watson, J. C., & Rennie, D. L. (1994). Qualitative analysis of clients' subjective experience of significant moments during the exploration of problematic reactions. *Journal of Counseling Psychology*, 41, 500-509.

Weick, K. (1995). *Sense-making in organizations*. Thousand Oaks, CA: Sage.

White, M., & Epston, D. (1990). *Narrative means to therapeutic ends*. New York: Norton.

Winnicott, D. (1969). The use of an object. *International Journal of Psycho-analysis. 50*, 711-716.

About the Author

Mark L. Savickas is Professor Emeritus of Family and Community Medicine and Chair Emeritus of the Behavioral Sciences Department at the Northeast Ohio Medical University. He is also an Adjunct Professor of Counselor Education at Kent State University. His website is www.Vocopher.com.

www.ingramcontent.com/pod-product-compliance
Lightning Source LLC
Chambersburg PA
CBHW050551280326
41933CB00011B/1806